Grandmothers at Work

Meet My Grandmother

She's a Children's Book Author

By Lisa Tucker McElroy
(with help from
Abigail Jane Cobb)

Photographs by Joel Benjamin

THE MILLBROOK PRESS
BROOKFIELD, CONNECTICUT

For my editor, mentor, and friend, Jean Reynolds, who came up with the idea for this book. Jean, thank you for all that you do.

ACKNOWLEDGMENTS

Dan Norman; Steve McElroy; Zoe McElroy; Matthew Sperber, Director and Valerie G. Annis, Children's Services Librarian, The Brookfield Library, Brookfield, CT; Jean Reynolds; Amy Shields; Ginger Giles; Mary Ellen Casey; Judie Mills; City Limits Restaurant, White Plains, NY; Ned Stuart; Barbara Lavallee; My Dollhouse, Nyack, NY; Theo and Rachel Cobb; Valerie Annis and Dan Annis; Kathy Darling; Todd Shapiro; Rick Goldstein; and Erminia Forcellati.

All photos by Joel Benjamin with the exception of the following: Courtesy of Vicki Cobb, p. 4 left top and bottom; p. 13 both; p. 15; p. 20; p. 21; p. 22; p.23. Courtesy of Valerie Annis, p. 14; Courtesy of Dan Annis, p. 25.

On p. 9, text from YOU GOTTA TRY THIS by Vicki Cobb and Kathy Darling. Text copyright © 1999 by Vicki Cobb and Kathy Darling, illustrations copyright © 1999 by True Kelley. Used by permission of HarperCollins Publishers. p. 12 top, illustration copyright © 2001 by Cynthia C. Lewis from FEELING YOUR WAY: DISCOVER YOUR SENSE OF TOUCH by Vicki Cobb, published by Millbrook Press, Inc.; p. 12 bottom illustration copyright © 2001 by Steve Haefele from BANGS AND TWANGS: SCIENCE FUN WITH SOUND by Vicki Cobb, published by Millbrook Press, Inc.

Library of Congress Cataloging-in-Publication Data
McElroy, Lisa Tucker.
Meet my grandmother. She's a children's book author / by Lisa Tucker McElroy
(with help from Abigail Jane Cobb); photographs by Joel Benjamin.
p. cm. – (Grandmothers at work)
ISBN 0-7613-1972-7 (lib. bdg.)
1. Cobb, Vicki—Juvenile literature. 2. Science writers—United States—Biography—Juvenile literature.
3. Children's literature—Authorship—Juvenile literature. [1. Cobb, Vicki. 2. Authors, American. 3. Women—
Biography. 4. Children's writings.] I. Cobb, Abigail Jane. II. Benjamin, Joel, ill. III. Title.
Q143.C59 M34 2001 509.2—dc21 [B] 00-067872

Published by The Millbrook Press, Inc.
2 Old New Milford Road, Brookfield, Connecticut 06804
www.millbrookpress.com

Take a leaf blower, some toilet paper,

a broomstick, and lots of energy, and what do you have? My grandmother's job! Gran spends her days doing things like blowing toilet paper around and setting tea bags on fire. Even though it might sound like she's destroying things, she's really trying out science experiments for her books. My name is Abby Cobb, and I'm nine years old. My grandmother, Vicki Cobb, is a children's book author.

3

Even though Gran has had lots of different jobs—she's been a teacher, a scientist, and a television writer—what she really loves to do is write about science. Believe it or not, she's written more than eighty science books for kids! She's been writing them ever since her sons, my dad and Uncle Josh, were little. When they were kids, they liked reading them. Now she counts on me to give her my opinion. I like the books about the five senses best.

Can you find Gran in these old photos? (Answer: Gran is the second one from the back in the top photo and the woman seated on the left in the bottom one.)

Most people can't go to work in their pajamas, but Gran could if she wanted to (although she would have to get dressed before she headed outside with the leaf blower)! That's because she works at home. She has a big office in the basement of her condo near New York City. It's full of books—both hers and other people's—and things she uses for science experiments. It also has all kinds of high-tech equipment. Gran loves scanners and computers and color copiers and cameras and stuff like that! She even has her own Web page: www.vickicobb.com. It's got all kinds of information about her books and science. What's really neat is that my dad designed her Web page for her!

Gran's office looks out

over a really pretty duck pond. If it's a nice day when I'm visiting her, we like to go out there and feed the ducks or have a snack on the patio.

My favorite snack is chocolate pie, but the ducks like stale bread best.

Gran also works in her kitchen when she's doing science experiments, especially edible ones. Some of Gran's first books were about science experiments you can eat, and she loves to come up with ideas for new experiments while she's cooking. She puts illustrations on her refrigerator from books she's working on so that she can think about them over lunch or while she chops vegetables.

Lots of Gran's books—like the one you can see the title page for on the refrigerator—have funny names. She has a great time coming up with them.

Gran's assistant, Ned, helps her stay organized and focused. Her coauthor, Kathy, helps her have fun!

You might think that writing a book

is sort of a lonely thing to do, but Gran works with lots of other people.
She has coauthors, or people who write books with her. Gran likes it
when she gets a chance to work with other authors. She says that they
give her good ideas and help her improve her writing. When they help her
with experiments, they get a few good laughs!

I have fun, too, doing

experiments from Gran's books.
Sucking liquid through a straw is
usually pretty easy. But it gets hard-
er when you try to drink through a
really long straw. You've got to have
real lung power to suck soda
through five straws, like I did here.
I had to stand on a chair to be able
to do it!

A REALLY BiG SUCKER

Suck through an extremely long straw.

Find out how big a sucker you are. Can you drink through a one-foot straw? A two footer? A five footer? If you're good, you may have to stand on a chair!

You will need:
• plastic straws
• scissors
• tape
• a beverage

To test your pucker power, make a maxistraw by joining plastic straws together. Because it is important that you get an airtight seal, make two half-inch slits in one of each straw. Mesh the

straws at the slits so that they overlap. Then tape the joint securely.

Start testing your lung power with a three-piece straw. Put it into your beverage and suck away. If you get a few good swallows, add another straw. Keep adding straws until you reach your limit. Vicki's last straw was number six. Kathy was not as big a sucker.

two ½-inch slits in one end of each straw

Overlap the straws then tape the joint.

When I visit Gran, I always ask her to do her flying tea bag experiment. You have to open the top of a tea bag and empty the tea out and then open the bottom of the bag so that it forms a paper tube. Then you put the tube on a plate and light the top on fire. Watch as the fire travels from the top of the tea bag to the bottom.

When it reaches the bottom, the tea bag will fly! Gran says that it happens because hot air rises, cool air rushes in to replace the rising column of warmer air, and a convection current forms. I promised her that I would never do this experiment without an adult with me.

10

 The little kid in the picture above my head is me when I was a baby!

11

Gran also works with illustrators,

or people who draw the pictures for her books. My dad has illustrated a couple of books for her! Lots of people think that children's book authors have to write and do the illustrations for their books, but that's not true. Usually, one person draws the pictures and another person writes the words, called text. That's a good thing, because Gran is a great writer, but she's not as good at drawing. I'm the one who loves to draw. I'm always telling Gran that I'll illustrate her books for her when I grow up!

Yup, the lady in the illustration on the right is Gran! The kid in the other one doesn't look much like me, though.

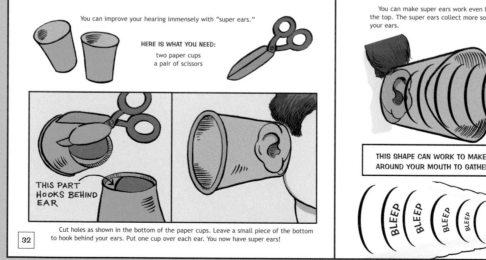

You can improve your hearing immensely with "super ears."

HERE IS WHAT YOU NEED:
two paper cups
a pair of scissors

THIS PART HOOKS BEHIND EAR

Cut holes as shown in the bottom of the paper cups. Leave a small piece of the bottom to hook behind your ears. Put one cup over each ear. You now have super ears!

32

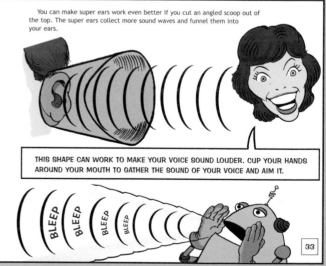

You can make super ears work even better if you cut an angled scoop out of the top. The super ears collect more sound waves and funnel them into your ears.

THIS SHAPE CAN WORK TO MAKE YOUR VOICE SOUND LOUDER. CUP YOUR HANDS AROUND YOUR MOUTH TO GATHER THE SOUND OF YOUR VOICE AND AIM IT.

BLEEP BLEEP BLEEP BLEEP

33

Gran likes to see the places she writes about, so for her geography books, she has traveled around the world with her friend Barbara. They have gone on some really cool trips—to Japan, to the equator, to Australia. For example, for Gran's book *This Place Is High*, they went to the Andes mountains, and for *This Place Is Cold*, they went to Alaska. When Gran wrote about ice cream, she visited a dairy farm and an ice-cream factory (yum!). When she wrote about sneakers, she went to a sneaker factory to see how soles were made and laces were strung.

Turkey

Australia

13

Gran loves to bring me dolls from the places she visits. I have a pretty big collection. She also brings me clothes and jewelry and musical instruments to teach me about other places and cultures.

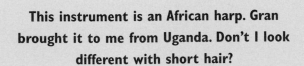

★

This instrument is an African harp. Gran brought it to me from Uganda. Don't I look different with short hair?

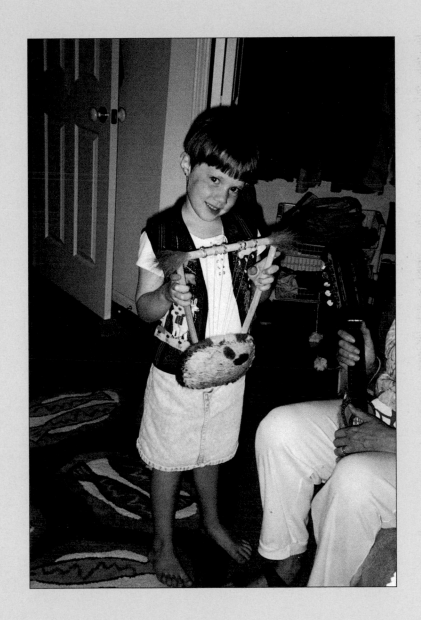

Sometimes ideas for books just pop into Gran's head, and sometimes she will read an article or notice something happening that inspires her. She says that she's always looking for the science in ordinary life. She likes it when other people suggest ideas to her, too. When she gets a good idea, she calls her agent, who is the person in charge of helping Gran find publishers for her books. Then her agent sends the idea to an editor, who is the person who works with authors at a publishing house. If an editor likes the idea, he or she will work with the agent to draw up a contract for Gran to write the book. The contract says how long the book will be, what it will be about, who will do the illustrations, and how much Gran will get paid.

Once Gran has a contract, she starts the research for the book. Sometimes the research takes a long time, like if Gran has to visit a faraway place. Sometimes she can do the research pretty quickly if it just involves doing science experiments at home.

Then Gran sits down to write the book. She likes to write at her computer in her office. Writing the book can take a few weeks or many months, depending on how long and complicated it is. It's a full-time job for Gran! Usually, Gran writes at least two or three books a year.

Several times a year, Gran goes to visit her editor and publisher so that they can talk about the books she's working on and help her come up with ideas for new ones. Even though Gran has been writing for a long time, her editor and publisher always have good suggestions for ways to improve her books. Gran usually makes a lot of changes to the text—or the manuscript—after one of these meetings. She's always happier with her books afterward! She says that even the best authors need to listen to what their editors say, because editors are great at reading manuscripts and figuring out what parts are perfect and what parts need to be clearer or more interesting. No author gets a book just right on the first try.

Gran's editor likes to show Gran
the illustrations for new books and
have Gran write captions and new
text to go with them.

Gran's publisher talks with Gran
about what new books Gran would
like to write.

19

Another really important part of Gran's job is her presentations at schools. Gran travels to schools across the country to talk with kids about her books and about science. Her programs are called "Science Surprises," and the kids love them! She even did one at my school last year. For each "Science Surprise," Gran talks about what it's like to write books for a living and shows the kids some science experiments.

The kids at the schools Gran visits usually make neat signs to welcome her. Gran always asks someone to take a photo of her with the displays.

Gran loves to do fun science experiments and sign books for her fans. The kids learn a lot about science from her programs, and their teachers pick up some ideas about teaching science, too.

When Gran does Science Surprises, the kids always have a lot of questions for Gran about her work.

21

Gran says that becoming a grandmother was one of the most exciting things that has ever happened to her! I was her first grandchild, and she tried to be there for my birth. My mom was supposed to have me any minute, and Gran was in town for one day for a school program. Gran made my mom walk around and around the shopping mall so that maybe I would be born before she left! It worked, but not in time. Gran had to leave for another school program, and she got a message from my dad that I had been born a few hours later. Luckily, she was able to come see me the next week. She thought I was so cute, she spent a lot of time visiting after that.

Gran might have been excited when I was born, but I was really excited when she got married! Several years ago, Gran was doing a school program in Vail, Colorado. She made sure that she went in the winter, because she loves to ski. As she was skiing down the slopes, she saw a man in a big silver top hat. They rode the ski lift together, and a few years later, they got married! My little sister Lexie and I got to shop for special dresses for the wedding, and we had a great time.

I live in Racine, Wisconsin, so Gran only visits a few times a year, but when we get together, we have a million things to do! We love to paint doll-house furniture, do science experiments, and write books. A few years ago, when I visited her at her house, we wrote a book called *Abby's Excellent Adventure in New York.*

It was so much fun! It made me feel like I might want to be a writer when I grow up.

Gran also loves to visit me when I have something special going on at school. Last year, I was in the school variety show. I dressed up like Dorothy from *The Wizard of Oz* and sang "Over the Rainbow." Gran said that there was no way she was going to miss that, so she listened to me practice over the phone long-distance, then she came to Wisconsin to put my hair in pigtails for me and to see the show.

Every summer, my mom and dad take Lexie and me to visit Gran and Poppy. They live near New York City. This year, I got to spend a couple of days with Gran all by myself after Lexie and my parents went home. We had an awesome time!

First, we went to the dollhouse store. Gran got me a dollhouse kit a few years ago, and I know I can make my dollhouse beautiful. We looked at rugs and lamps and dishes. I also wanted a new dollhouse family, as mine is starting to look pretty worn-out. Lexie needed a bathroom set for her dollhouse, so Gran and I picked one out.

After shopping, Gran and I headed out to lunch.
We both love eating out! There's this really cool diner near where Gran
lives, and it's one of our favorite places. It looks like something out of the
1950s, or so Gran tells me. Gran made the ketchup come out too fast all
over my hamburger, but, other than that, we had a great lunch!

After lunch, we went swimming. There's a great pool in Gran's condo complex. I had to talk Gran into putting on her suit and going for a swim with me. I promised not to splash, a promise I tried to keep, but . . . . Lucky for me, Gran has a good sense of humor about these things.

A few years ago, Gran was at a conference for people who love books. She was standing near a stack of her books, and a little girl and her mom came up to look at them. When the little girl picked up a book and started to read, Gran didn't tell them that she was the author; she just stood and watched. Even when the mother said it was time to go, the little girl begged to stay. She said it was such a good book that she wanted to finish it! Gran says that was when she really knew she had the best job in the world.

After all, how many people get to blow
toilet paper around and call it work?

If You Want to Be a Children's Book Author . . .

Take every opportunity to write. Many authors keep journals, write poetry, or even just e-mail their friends about interesting things they've done. All kinds of writing are good practice.

Read a lot, and read critically. You have to read what other people are writing in order to come up with original, interesting ideas that will appeal to kids.

Think about what it's like to be a kid. Only kids and adults who can talk to kids in their own language, about issues that interest them, write good children's books.

Don't be afraid to listen to constructive criticism and rewrite your work. Every author writes several drafts of her books, and the books usually improve with each re-write!

Try to notice what's interesting in everyday life. Most children's books center around an ordinary concept that becomes interesting and extraordinary because of the author's unique perspective.

Write about things you know. If you live in Wisconsin, don't write about what it's like to be a kid in Alaska. If you're crazy about computers, write about kids who use computers, not kids who ice skate or kids who like stamp collecting. Your enthusiasm and knowledge will make your books interesting.

Learn to be punctual. Books are produced on a schedule, and your book, however good, won't get published if you don't get it to your editor on time!

Collaborate with a friend who's good at drawing or photography. Great illustrations or photographs can make your book come alive!

Be patient. It takes about eighteen months from the time you finish writing a book for it to make it to the library and bookstore shelves. Imagine what a great day it will be when you see your name in print on a book's cover!